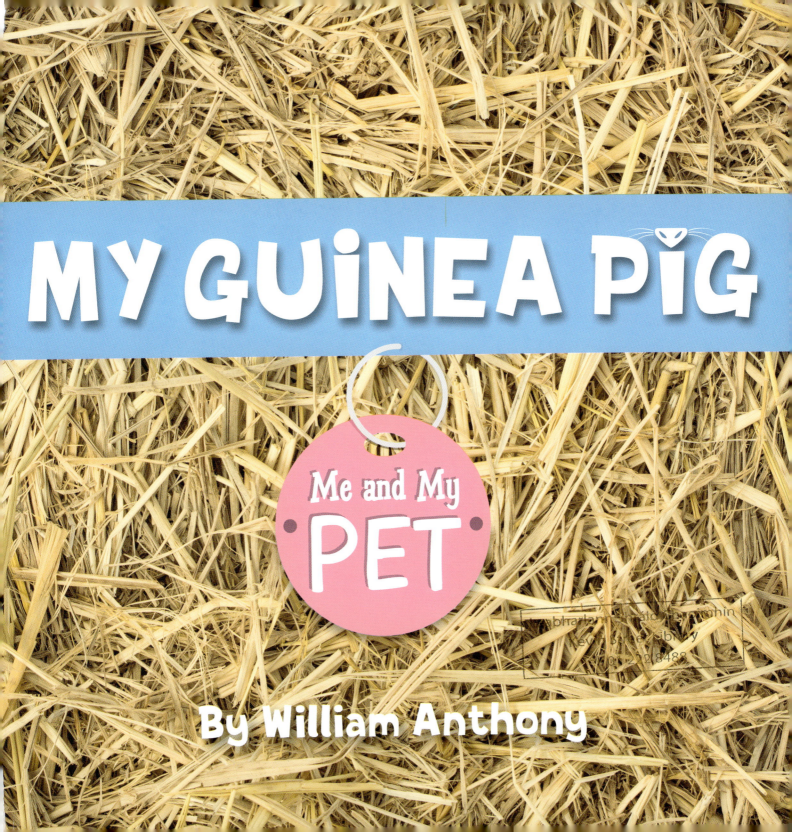

# MY GUINEA PIG

## Me and My PET

## By William Anthony

# BookLife
## PUBLISHING

©2019
**BookLife Publishing Ltd.**
**King's Lynn**
**Norfolk PE30 4LS**

All rights reserved.
Printed in Malaysia.

A catalogue record for this book is available from the British Library.

**ISBN:** 978-1-78637-575-9

**Written by:**
William Anthony

**Edited by:**
Madeline Tyler

**Designed by:**
Jasmine Pointer

# CONTENTS

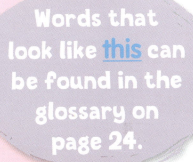

Words that look like this can be found in the glossary on page 24.

# Zoe ♥ and Fudge

Hello! My name's Zoe, and this is my pet guinea pig, Fudge. He's four years old. He has a friend called Sherbet. They live together because guinea pigs like living in **pairs**!

Zoe

Fudge

4

I think Sherbet's sleeping at the moment, so it looks like it will be just me and Fudge talking you through how to look after guinea pigs!

Lead the way, Fudge!

# Getting Guinea Pigs

Looking after guinea pigs means you are going to have a lot of **responsibility**. You will need to feed them, and give them a nice home with lots of space.

My family got Fudge and Sherbet from a pet shop, but you can also get guinea pigs from a **rescue centre** or from a breeder. A breeder is someone who keeps guinea pigs to **mate** them.

Remember, it's best to keep guinea pigs in pairs, so be ready to look after two animals!

7

# Home

If you keep your guinea pig outside, make sure their home is warm and out of the wind.

Guinea pigs don't like loud noises. If your house is noisy, it might be a good idea to keep them outside.

They will need a cage with lots of space for exercise and a good **shelter** where they can sleep. You could get them tunnels for their cage to keep them entertained.

# Playtime

Guinea Pig Run

Most guinea pigs have fun exploring. You could also get them a **run** so they can explore safely in your garden.

When you're playing with your guinea pigs, you must be very calm and gentle. Guinea pigs don't like loud noises so don't shout when you're petting them.

# Food

Guinea pigs need food to stay alive, just like us. They are easy animals to feed. Guinea pigs need lots of hay and some pellet food, which you can get from any pet shop.

Pellet Food

Guinea pigs need different types of food in their diet.

You can also give your guinea pigs different types of vegetables. They like things like carrots, broccoli and cabbage. This keeps their diets healthy and balanced.

# Bedtime

Sherbet is still asleep; shall we take a quick peek?
He's sleeping on a soft and fluffy blanket. Guinea pigs
also like to sleep on soft paper or wood shavings.

Sorry Sherbet, did we wake you up? We'll move on and let you get back to sleep! Guinea pigs usually have short naps, so he'll be awake again soon.

Yawwnn!

15

# The Vet

Vets are like doctors, but for animals instead of humans!

Guinea pigs can get ill, just like humans. Guinea pigs that are ill can go to the vets. The vet will do everything they can to help your guinea pig get better again!

One day when I came home, Fudge was sneezing and had crusty eyes. I told my parents and we took him to the vet, who made him all better again!

If you think your guinea pig isn't very well, make sure you tell an adult.

# Growing Up

When guinea pigs get older, they find it hard to move as quickly as they used to. It's important to be gentle with older guinea pigs.

You could also try to make their cage more comfortable. Make sure they can reach their water easily, and have somewhere soft to rest and sleep.

You could even bring your elderly guinea pig indoors to help them stay warm.

# Super Guinea Pigs

Normal guinea pigs are amazing, but some guinea pigs are simply super. A guinea pig called Truffles holds the world record for the farthest jump by a guinea pig. He jumped 48 centimetres!

That's farther than two pages of this book!

Wow!

ZOOM!

Another guinea pig, called Flash, holds the world record for the fastest 10-metre run. He ran it in just under nine seconds.

# You ❤ and Your Pet

Whether you have a young guinea pig, an old guinea pig or a super guinea pig, make sure you take care of them just like Fudge and I have taught you!

I'm sure you'll make a great pet owner. I hope your new furry friend enjoys their new home, and that you have lots of fun together.

# GLOSSARY

| | |
|---|---|
| **balanced** | having good or equal amounts of something |
| **diet** | the kind of food that an animal or person usually eats |
| **mate** | to produce young with an animal of the same species |
| **pairs** | two of something |
| **rescue centre** | a place that helps animals that have had a difficult life find a new loving home |
| **responsibility** | having tasks that you are expected to do |
| **run** | a safe enclosure that lets animals explore different areas while staying safe |
| **shelter** | something that covers or protects people or things |

# INDEX